The Emotional Literacy Toolkit for ADHD

from the author

The Teenage Girl's Guide to Living Well with ADHD
Improve your Self-Esteem, Self-Care and Self Knowledge
Sonia Ali
ISBN 978 1 78775 768 4
eISBN 978 1 78775 769 1

of related interest

Emotion Coaching with Children and Young People in Schools
Promoting Positive Behavior, Wellbeing and Resilience
Louise Gilbert, Licette Gus and Janet Rose
Foreword by John Gottman, Ph.D.
ISBN 978 1 78775 798 1
eISBN 978 1 78775 799 8

Using Picture Books to Enhance Children's Social and Emotional Literacy
Creative Activities and Programs for Parents and Professionals
Susan Elswick
ISBN 978 1 78592 737 9
eISBN 978 1 78450 451 9

THE EMOTIONAL LITERACY TOOLKIT FOR ADHD

Strategies for Better Emotional Regulation and Peer Relationships in Children and Teens

SONIA ALI

Illustrated by Tim Stringer

Jessica Kingsley Publishers
London and Philadelphia

First published in Great Britain in 2024 by Jessica Kingsley Publishers
An imprint of Hodder & Stoughton Ltd
An Hachette Company

1

A CIP catalogue record for this title is available from the
British Library and the Library of Congress

ISBN 978 1 83997 426 7
eISBN 978 1 83997 427 4

Printed and bound in Great Britain by TJ Books Ltd

Jessica Kingsley Publishers' policy is to use papers that are natural, renewable
and recyclable products and made from wood grown in sustainable
forests. The logging and manufacturing processes are expected to
conform to the environmental regulations of the country of origin.

Jessica Kingsley Publishers
Carmelite House
50 Victoria Embankment
London EC4Y 0DZ

www.jkp.com

MIX
Paper from
responsible sources
FSC
www.fsc.org   FSC® C013056

Contents

Introduction for the Mentor

The background

For some young people with ADHD, emotion and mood regulation can be challenging. In a study of 1500 children with ADHD, challenges with emotional regulation were found to have a far greater impact on self-esteem and mood than challenges with hyperactivity and attention regulation.[1]

Many young people with ADHD experience:

- **heightened emotional reactivity** – emotional reactions that are disproportionate to the situation, such as outbursts of extreme anger

- **rejection sensitivity** – a heightened sensitivity to criticism, perceived or otherwise

- **irritability and low frustration levels** – difficulty managing feelings of frustration which may result in abrupt mood changes

- **increased conflict with others**

- **social anxiety,** culminating in withdrawal from some social situations.

Emotional regulation and peer relationships

A child or young person who finds it very difficult to regulate strong emotions, such as anger, will often find that they experience increased conflict and misunderstanding in their interpersonal relationships. A recent review of peer relationships and friendships in youth with ADHD found that amongst some young people with ADHD peer difficulties often arise.[2]

The purpose of this book

This book was devised to support the teaching of emotional literacy skills for young people with ADHD (diagnosed or not), and some young people with a dual diagnosis of ADHD and autism, between the ages of 11 and 17.

There is clear evidence that effective psychoeducation to boost self-knowledge and mentoring to support the development of emotional literacy skills can positively affect a young person's ability to understand and regulate their emotions.

While ADHD may increase an individual's susceptibility to sudden and powerful emotional reactions that 'flood' their nervous system, a young person can mitigate the more stressful effects of this emotional 'flooding' by developing the following knowledge and skills:

- a better understanding of themselves and what triggers heightened emotional reactions

- an improved ability to recognize the physical and physiological signs that indicate emotional dysregulation and stress

- strategies to stay safe and self-soothe to minimize harmful or destructive behaviours when in a heightened state

- an improved ability to recognize early signs of stress and burnout so as to implement healthy coping strategies

- a better understanding of how to implement self-care and seek support to maintain emotional and physical health

- tools to resolve conflict with others.

The importance of co-regulation

It is important to note that the success of any emotional literacy intervention is also dependent on the capacity of the adults in the young person's life to co-regulate and find ways to support their emotional well-being.

Effective emotion regulation modelled by the adults around them, most of the time, and school-based accommodations that support the young person's learning profile, will help to embed the strategies adopted from this book.

What is the role of the Mentor?

The aim of this book is for the young person to better understand, process and regulate their strong emotions and not to suppress them. *As the Mentor, your role is to guide the young person through the questions and exercises and provide the opportunity for discussion and reflection during and after each chapter.*

Each chapter in this book begins with learning objectives, which make it clear what the young person can expect to gain from working through the chapter. There then follows an explanatory or informative script that can be read by the Mentor or the young person, or both together.

The main body of the chapter includes questions to discuss, as well as cartoons or brief scenarios to encourage reflection and discussion. There are also activities, such as questionnaires or multiple-choice quizzes, which encourage the young person to reflect on their own experiences and feelings, and there are tools designed to help with the types of feelings and situations discussed. *You, the Mentor, will lead on these activities and questions and prompt the young person to elaborate or reflect on their answers.*

How to use this book

This book was not written to be followed prescriptively. It is not necessary to follow the support sessions in a strict order or within a strict time-frame.

Time constraints in school or at home mean that it may be challenging sometimes to schedule and allocate a specific amount of time at regular intervals during the week.

It is entirely appropriate to use the book in any of the following ways:

- Read and follow the exercises in one chapter and allow a few weeks to discuss and reflect on how these skills have been embedded and practised in real-life situations.

- Prioritize chapters that are most relevant to the profile of the student and work through those only.

- Use the book as a reference and 'tool box' to support specific skills as and when they become pertinent.

The questionnaire in the introduction will help you and the young person you are working with identify the chapters that are most relevant to them. It could be helpful to read the chapters first before working with a young person, so you can think about how much time you will take on the activities.

The exercises in this book can be worked through with a pencil, pen and paper or journal, and interactive copies of some of the longer activities, indicated with ⭐, are available to download at https://www.jkp.com/catalogue/book/9781839974267.

ADHD and trauma – When is therapeutic intervention necessary?

Challenges with emotional regulation can also be evident in young people who have experienced trauma and/or poor attachment. Children with ADHD who have experienced adverse childhood experiences may have a harder time regulating their emotions than those who have not had these experiences.

Arguably, a neurodivergent young person may have an increased likelihood of experiencing some type of childhood adversity, such as social isolation or bullying, which can be internalized as trauma.

It is possible that emotional dysregulation is a sign of co-occurring mental health difficulties that require more intensive therapeutic intervention from mental health services.

It is important to note that this book is not a therapeutic intervention.

Any young person showing any of the signs listed below should be referred for assessment by Child and Adolescent Mental Health Services (CAMHS) to receive appropriate therapeutic support as soon as possible:

- persistent low mood or moderate to severe anxiety
- challenges with emotional regulation that are not improving or are worsening
- self-harm and suicidal ideation
- disordered eating
- substance abuse
- harmful sexual behaviour.

The following links on the NSPCC website outline the key signs to look for that may indicate that a child is experiencing a mental health difficulty.

- Signs that a child or young person is experiencing anxiety or depression:

  www.nspcc.org.uk/keeping-children-safe/childrens-mental-health/depression-anxiety-mental-health

- Signs that a child is self-harming and how to keep them safe:

  www.nspcc.org.uk/keeping-children-safe/childrens-mental-health/self-harm

Introduction: What Is 'Emotional Literacy'?

When you have ADHD, you may feel that your emotions can become very intense, quite suddenly. If you are excited or happy, this can be fantastic, but if you become angry, the intensity of your rage may overwhelm your capacity to think clearly before acting.

Developing your emotional literacy can help you find ways to return to a regulated state even when you are very angry.

Take a look at the comic strip below. **What do you think happened during and after the game? How did Jack's emotional reaction affect the game?**

How does ADHD affect your thinking?

When you have ADHD, your mind can get very busy with hundreds of thoughts and ideas swirling around during the day.

A restless mind may help you to generate new ideas or be creative, but it can also lead you to ruminate or dwell on problems or to think negative thoughts that distort your perception of events. Emotional literacy can help you understand the link between your thoughts and your mood and learn ways to manage negative and intrusive thoughts.

So, what *is* emotional literacy?

The word 'literacy' is often associated with reading and writing, but literacy has another meaning – it means to be skilled at something. You can be 'computer literate' or 'maths literate', for example.

Emotional literacy includes: skills in understanding your emotions and the underlying reasons behind them; recognizing when your emotions are very heightened and having the tools to return to a regulated state more quickly; or tolerating situations that might have previously overwhelmed you.

Increased emotional literacy is associated with better mental and physical health as well as more secure self-esteem.

What do you think could be helpful for you about learning about emotional literacy?

EMOTIONAL LITERACY: A QUESTIONNAIRE

Read through each statement below and note how many statements you agree or somewhat agree with.

If you find you agree or somewhat agree with nearly all the statements in a section, begin working through the chapters recommended.

Self-esteem and self-knowledge

1. **I would like to understand why I get very angry or nervous in some situations**

2. **I am hyper-sensitive about how others perceive me**

3. **I would like to become less angry or nervous in some situations that 'trigger' this reaction**

4. **I would like to understand what I can do to feel less tense sometimes**

5. **I find it hard to get enough sleep**

6. **I don't really understand how sensory or environmental factors affect my stress levels**

Questions 1 to 3: Mostly *agree* or *somewhat agree?*
Read Chapter 1: The Protective Power of Self-Esteem

This chapter explores something called the fight or flight response and will help you understand why we can become angry or scared in situations that are not overtly threatening.

This chapter will also help you think of ways to build a more secure self-esteem that is less dependent on external validation.

Questions 4 to 6: Mostly agree or somewhat agree?
Read Chapter 2: How to Increase Your Window of Tolerance

In Chapter 2, you will learn about a concept called the Window of Tolerance. When you are in your Window of Tolerance, you feel more able to handle stress or difficult situations. In this chapter we think about the sorts of steps you can take to help you stay in your Window of Tolerance, including environmental changes and daily habits.

Managing negative or intrusive thoughts

7. **My thoughts sometimes make me feel very anxious or worried, and I don't know what to do about it**

8. **I often compare myself to others**

9. **I would like to learn some ways to recognize and manage negative thoughts**

Questions 7 to 9: Mostly agree or somewhat agree?
Read Chapter 3: Self-Care for Your Busy Mind: How to Regulate and Manage Your Thoughts to Stay in Your Window of Tolerance

Chapter 3 explores the link between your thinking and emotions. In this chapter, you can learn what to do when you notice your thinking is causing you distress and making you feel low or worried.

Regulating anger and resolving conflict

10. **I find it very hard to control my anger at times**

11. **I don't always understand why I become so angry**

12. **I think it could be useful to learn ways to regulate anger**

13. **I can be quite argumentative**

14. **I don't really know how to resolve a disagreement without arguing and getting angry**

15. **It could be helpful to learn different approaches to resolve a disagreement with someone**

Questions 10 to 12: *Mostly agree or somewhat agree?*
Read Chapter 4: Tips to Manage Rage

Chapter 4 explores some common triggers for rage. You will learn techniques to help you feel regulated, such as RADE.

Questions 13 to 15: *Mostly agree or somewhat agree?*
Read Chapter 5: Conflict Resolution

In this chapter, you will learn about different approaches to conflict resolution and how to resolve or repair a situation after anger has subsided.

We will consider when it can be helpful to consider another person's viewpoint and when we should seek support or the intervention of a third party.

Managing anxiety and overwhelm

16. **I can get very nervous or stressed in social situations**

17. **I sometimes worry too much about how others might perceive me and this makes me nervous**

18. **I would like to find ways to feel less worried or panicked in situations involving other people**

19. **I sometimes get so stressed and overwhelmed in the morning that I cry or don't want to leave the house**

20. **I often feel overwhelmed by all the things that I have to do**

21. **I would like to find coping strategies to help when I feel overwhelmed**

Questions 16 to 18: Mostly *agree* or *somewhat agree?*
Read Chapter 6: Social Anxiety: What to Do When You Feel Under the Spotlight

In this chapter we will explore why we can feel anxious in certain social situations and learn three steps that we can take to gradually improve social anxiety.

Questions 19 to 21: Mostly *agree* or *somewhat agree?*
Read Chapter 7: Overwhelm: How to Manage That Monday Morning Panic

In this chapter, you will reflect on the situations or experiences that might prompt you to feel overwhelmed and learn about the START technique to help you return to your Window of Tolerance.

Recognizing and managing stress

22. **I don't really know how to gauge when I am stressed or burnt out until I become overwhelmed**

23.I would like to learn different techniques that help me to de-stress and feel more relaxed

24.I often use screen time well into the night to unwind

Questions 22 to 24: Mostly *agree* or somewhat *agree*?
Read Chapter 8: Become a CAMPER and Manage Stress

This helps you spot early signs of stress and burnout before you get too overwhelmed. You will learn self-care strategies that help you recover from the stress of feeling burnt out, using the CAMPER approach.

Chapter 1

THE PROTECTIVE POWER OF SELF-ESTEEM

LEARNING OBJECTIVES

☆ Learn about the fight or flight response and what can trigger this response

☆ Learn how to maintain secure self-esteem to minimize perceiving threat in particular situations

What do you think is the same and different about each of these images?

It is easy to figure out why the person in the first image is terrified... there is a large, angry dog chasing them! **But the person in the second image is not in any obvious danger, so why do you think they are feeling scared?**

The fight or flight response to threat

We experience fear or anger when we perceive any kind of threat.

When we recognize a threat, our nervous system often activates a physiological response called the fight or flight response.

In fight or flight, the hormone adrenaline is released into our body, increasing our heart rate and the blood flow pumping through our muscles to prepare our body for action.

The hormone cortisol is also released. It helps speed up our thinking, *and* gives us faster reaction times, to help us defend ourselves or run.

The fight or flight response is our very own self-defence system, designed to equip us to handle dangerous situations, but it can be very stressful and exhausting to experience the fight or flight response often and in everyday situations.

Below are some examples of the physiological reactions we can experience in a fight or flight response. **Can you think of any others?**

- **Your heart beats really strongly** – it feels like it will burst out of your chest.

- **Your palms get very sweaty.**

- **Your head feels tight.**

What do you think could be a negative impact of experiencing the fight or flight response often?

Why might we experience the fight or flight response when there is no obvious danger?

You can perceive a threat from something in the external world, like a volcanic eruption or a wild animal chasing us, but it could also be from something fairly ordinary, like meeting new people or coming to school with a new haircut.

It's pretty obvious why we would perceive a wild animal chasing us as a threat, but why might meeting new people feel daunting for some?

The person in the second image is in fight or flight mode because they fear being judged or not accepted by a group of new people and feeling bad about themselves. They may have thoughts circling around their head that maximize this feeling of fear, such as *'What if I say something silly?'* or *'What if I feel really awkward?'*

They are not in physical danger, but they perceive an emotional threat.

We can frequently enter fight or flight mode if we anticipate a risk of feeling hurt or bad about ourselves. This may occur when we *perceive* that we are:

- **being ridiculed or criticized or judged**

- **being treated unfairly or not listened to.**

Sometimes, what we fear doesn't need to actually happen for us to enter fight or flight mode. Fearing, anticipating or perceiving it happening can be enough to trigger a strong reaction.

Read George's statement below. **Why do you think he experiences fight or flight in the situation he describes?**

'When I was in primary school, I used to get teased quite a lot about how I looked, mainly because of my teeth. (I have braces now.) Now, I get really angry whenever I think anyone is making a joke about me, even if I know, deep down, it's harmless. Most of my classmates don't get worked up when someone cracks a joke, but I feel a kind of rising panic inside of me and I lash out.'

Why do you think George feels very sensitive about any 'joking around'?

Everyone experiences the fight or flight response at times, but certain past experiences can leave you more sensitive to signs of threat. For example, if you were picked on or had a negative experience with peers, if you felt you were treated unfairly or ignored or if you experienced discrimination or difficult childhood experiences. You may be hypervigilant to signs of this happening again and become very angry and argue to protect yourself.

The freeze state

Someone who is often in a fight or flight state can become emotionally exhausted and numb. In this state, a person can find it hard to take any action and may even struggle to get out of bed or go out.

ADHD and 'rejection sensitivity'

Some people with ADHD may notice that they experience very intense feelings of hurt if they think someone is criticizing or rejecting them. This intense reaction to perceived criticism is sometimes called rejection sensitivity. Rejection sensitivity may be the result of hurtful past experiences, but it can also be because of differences in how the brain processes emotions.

Read through the statements below and note which ones you think apply to you.

- **I argue with other people more often than I probably need to.**

- **I get angry quickly if someone disagrees with me.**

- **If I meet someone new, I worry a lot about how I come across.**

- **I react quickly and strongly to the slightest hint of disrespect.**

- **I get very, very nervous about meeting new people.**

- **I am very sensitive to how others act towards me.**

- **I often look for ways that I am treated unfairly.**

If you identified with two or more of these statements, it could be a sign that you feel the need to defend yourself and are often in fight or flight mode.

The protective power of secure self-esteem

If you agreed with any of the statements you may be particularly sensitive to signs of rejection or criticism or disrespect. You may fear that the actions of others will trigger feelings of low self-worth.

One way to feel less easily triggered or sensitive to the reactions of others is to develop a more secure self-esteem.

What is 'secure' self-esteem?

Which of the statements below do you think best describes the meaning of self-esteem?

- **Secure self-esteem is feeling really confident all the time.**

- **Secure self-esteem is feeling that you are better than other people.**

- **Secure self-esteem is how you feel if you are very good at something.**

- **Secure self-esteem means you value and accept yourself.**

The final statement is the correct one.

Secure self-esteem is not about being good at everything or liked by everyone – it is about having an innate sense of self-worth and self-acceptance. If your self-esteem is secure, you may feel less threatened by the opinions of others. When you make a mistake or get something wrong, it is less likely to rock your sense of self and you will find it easier to bounce back. Having secure self-esteem may reduce the frequency with which you go into a fight or flight response.

SELF-ESTEEM CHECK

Before we explore what self-esteem is in more detail, it's a good idea to carry out a quick self-esteem check. Look at the questions and statements below and work through these.

Part One

1. **Say two positive things about yourself. This should be qualities that you feel that you have, rather than any achievements.**

2. **Now say two more positive things about yourself.**

3. **Now say another two more positive things about yourself.**

How easy was this for you to do? If you struggled to think of more than two positive things, then your self-esteem can be improved. The self-esteem action plan below will help you think of ways to improve how you value your unique qualities.

Part Two

1. **Have you ever done anything you were proud of? Can you describe what this was?**

2. **What do you think that you are fairly good at? (This does not need to be related to school or sport and can include anything; for example: being funny or being compassionate or fixing things.)**

3. **What are your interests? Name two or more activities or hobbies that you enjoy or find interesting. (Avoid passive activities like watching TV.)**

How did you do? Did you struggle with any question?

When we do activities that we find enjoyable and are interested in, we can enter 'flow state' where we are not consciously thinking of or worrying about things. This flow state improves our well-being and helps us feel good about ourselves. We often develop skills in areas that we enjoy too, so it can be a win-win situation.

If you found it difficult to answer these questions, it can be useful to begin to find out more about activities you might enjoy and feel you could be good at. In the self-esteem action plan, there will be the opportunity to think about creating these opportunities.

Part Three

Read these statements and say if they apply to you (**yes**, **no** or **sometimes**):

1. **I often get into arguments because I will never admit to being wrong.**

2. **I don't like to fail or make mistakes, so I avoid things that I will not be good at.**

3. **When I make mistakes, I can feel really bad.**

4. **I am very harsh about myself when I don't do well at something.**

5. **I often compare myself to people on social media and then I feel I bad about myself.**

Did you answer *yes* or *sometimes* to a few of these? Don't worry, many people would. If you agreed with two or more of these statements, your self-esteem might be contingent on you meeting certain criteria.

If you are very wary of making mistakes, being wrong or trying new things, your self-esteem may be too contingent on achievement or external validation. Many people confuse contingent self-esteem with secure self-esteem and constantly feel that they have to prove themselves.

When your self-esteem is too contingent on success or validation or personal achievement, if you don't do well or receive criticism, you may feel devastated. You may go to lengths to avoid situations where you are at risk of failing or making mistakes and can miss out on learning opportunities as a result.

What can be useful about making mistakes?

Self-esteem – how we perceive ourselves – begins to develop in early infancy and is shaped by the messages we receive about ourselves from family, peers, teachers and even the media. We cannot pretend that outside influences do not affect how we feel about ourselves, but there are ways that we can boost how we feel about ourselves.

CREATING A SELF-ESTEEM ACTION PLAN

Here are tips to support your self-esteem. It could be helpful to work through this with someone who can help you with some of the practical considerations.

Think kindly and compassionately about yourself

Sometimes, our self-talk can be very harsh and negative. We are often harder on ourselves than we would be to others. Chapter 3 explores the effects our thoughts can have on our emotions in more detail and will help you challenge negative thinking.

Try repeating any of these affirmations to yourself when you notice your self-talk is negative:

- **I am allowed to make mistakes and learn from them.**

- **I have positive qualities and strengths.**

- **I deserve to feel appreciated.**

- **I can ask for help when I need to.**

- **I don't need to be perfect.**

- **My unique qualities matter.**

Engage in activities and hobbies that you enjoy and help you learn new skills

If you already participate in activities that you really enjoy, then you can move on to the next step. If not:

- **Discuss with someone at school what extra-curricular activities you might be interested in trying. For example:**

  - *drama or other performing arts, such as dance*

  - *sports – football; athletics; basketball; swimming*

  - *art and craft activities*

  - *skateboarding or parkour.*

- **It might be useful to have a short chat about what kind of activities you think you have typically been interested in in the past. Are there any activities offered at your school that you might like to try? It can be a good idea to try a few activities to find an activity that is the 'right fit'.**

- **Set yourself goals that are not achievement-based, but are about learning or improving, such as *'I would like to learn karate'* or *'I want to improve my dancing'*.**

Spend time with people who you feel comfortable being around and appreciated by

If you spend time with people who frequently undermine you or are very critical, then this can eventually affect how you see yourself.

Sometimes, banter or joking around can become excessive; some people may point out flaws, but not encourage you. You cannot always control how others act, but you can communicate to them what is not acceptable and spend time with people who value you.

Look at the statements below and write down two or three more statements that are signs of good interpersonal relationships.

- **We will be honest, but won't bring each other down.**

- **We compromise sometimes and don't always do what one person wants.**

END-OF-CHAPTER THOUGHTS

Let's recap what we have explored so far.

☆ What is the fight or flight response?

☆ In what situations could the fight or flight response do us more harm than good?

☆ Why is building secure self-esteem helpful in emotional regulation?

☆ What is contingent self-esteem?

Chapter 2

HOW TO INCREASE YOUR WINDOW OF TOLERANCE

LEARNING OBJECTIVES

In this session, we are going to find out what Window of Tolerance means and learn three self-care strategies that can help you stay in your Window of Tolerance. These are good sleep, exercise and understanding how your environment affects you.

Look at the two images below. **What are the similarities and differences between them? What physiological and emotional responses do you think the people are having in each image?**

In the images, we see people in exactly the same environment, but they are having a completely different response to their environment.

Although the shopping centre looks very, very crowded and noisy, the person in the first image appears fairly calm and relaxed. They are in their Window of Tolerance.

In the second image, however, the person looks very stressed in this environment. They are definitely not in their Window of Tolerance.

What do you think is meant by the term Window of Tolerance?

The term Window of Tolerance was coined by Dr Dan Siegel MD to describe our optimum emotional and physiological state.[3] When we are in our Window of Tolerance, our physiological responses, such as our breathing and heart rate, are within a regular range. When we are in our Window of Tolerance it is easier for us to manage what is happening around us and to feel safe and secure; we may experience some stress which helps us perform certain tasks, but not so much that we are in a fight or flight state.

Are you within your Window of Tolerance now? How do you know?

When we are outside our Window of Tolerance, we are in a state of fight or flight. This is when our emotions and physiological responses are no longer regulated. In this state, our level of stress is far higher than is comfortable for us and we will experience extremes of anger (fight) or become very overwhelmed, anxious or panicked (flight). We will experience the following:

- an **increased heart rate**

- **muscle tightening**

- **short, shallow breathing**

- maybe even **crying or shouting.**

Everyone's Window of Tolerance can vary. Different situations can trigger a different response in people. In the previous chapter, we learnt about situations with other people that can lead us to feel threatened, but there are plenty of situations that cause us stress; for example:

Environmental stimuli – too noisy, smelly or busy?

There is a lot of sensory stimuli all around us. Some of us are particularly sensitive to sensory stimulation. If you have ADHD or are autistic, you may be very sensitive to sensory stimulation. This makes it harder to filter out all of the noise and textures and smells that are part of the environment. That means that a very busy crowded shopping centre could feel like an assault on your senses and even send you into a state of fight or flight.

Consider if any of these statements apply to you:

- **If I am in very busy and noisy places, I can feel overwhelmed and stressed.**

- **I find certain everyday smells so unbearable that I feel overwhelmed by them.**

- **At the end of a busy day, I feel very frazzled and irritable and need quiet time to decompress.**

- **I am quite sensitive to certain textures and I am**

very aware of things like the labels on my clothes or the feel of fabrics against my skin.

■ **Sometimes, certain background noises can be quite uncomfortable for me and make me agitated.**

If you are sensitive to sensory overwhelm from your environment, you can take certain steps that might minimize this feeling:

What can you do to minimize sensory overload?

Day-to-day

- **Many shops and shopping centres now have a quiet hour** for people who prefer calmer environments. If you need to do shopping, find out when these quieter times are.

- If you find that noises easily unsettle you, **you can use noise cancelling headphones in certain situations** (they look exactly like other headphones). **Is this something you might try?**

- **Gently explain to friends or relatives that certain smells can be difficult for you to manage and that you try to avoid them.**

- **Allow time after school to decompress;** think of a quiet spot in the house and explain to others that you need some time to regulate before you can join in with social activities. The last chapter in this book will explore things you can do to relax.

In school

- If lesson transitions are too noisy and busy in school, **you may be able to leave for your next lesson a little earlier to avoid moving around the school at busy times.** Speak to your SENCo (Special Educational Needs Coordinator).

- **During lessons, do you feel completely unable to process any more information?** Discuss with the SENCo in your school if you need **opportunities for a brain break** during the day.

- **Is there a calm place during break times or lunchtimes that you can go to when you feel overwhelmed?**

Sleep

Exhaustion and sleep deprivation have a huge impact on our mood and emotions and make us more likely to experience:

- **irritability and frustration**

- **mood swings and anger outbursts**

- **reduced concentration**

- **feelings of worry or low mood.**

If you have a mind that never stops ticking over, you will find it harder to relax and fall asleep. It may be too tempting to stay up late to engage in activities that you want to do.

Let's do a quick sleep questionnaire to find out what your sleep habits are like. Answer **yes**, **no** or **sometimes** to the statements below:

- **I tend to put off going to bed as long as possible.**

- **I find waking up really, really hard and often feel tired in the morning.**

- **At night, before bed, I often watch TV or scroll on my phone until just before lights out.**

- **After I do turn the lights out, it takes me a long time to fall asleep.**

- **I probably don't get enough sleep most nights.**

If you answered *no* to most of these, then we can skip the next section. If you answered *yes* to three or more, you are not alone. Many people have a delayed circadian rhythm, which means that they naturally want to fall asleep later. Unfortunately, most schools and colleges have early morning starts, so you can end up feeling exhausted if you stay up too late.

Tips that can help whatever your circadian rhythm

- After school, you probably want to spend as much time as possible watching TV, or scrolling, or messaging people, or doing something you like, but you can end up staying up too late. **Can you move everything forward an hour earlier?**

- **Get as much daylight and movement in during the day as possible.**

- Our circadian rhythm is programmed to respond to the light of day and the darkness of night. **Increasing your access to daylight can help regulate your circadian rhythm to this schedule.** Try to allow enough time to wind down before bed.

Can you guess what other activity helps sleep?

Exercise!

Exercise and movement

If you have ADHD, you have a busy mind and you are very motivated by new ideas and projects. Often this drive for novelty can lead to hyperactivity. Exercising and moving are key to helping keep your mind and body in a regulated state. The added bonus is that you can also become much fitter and healthier. Plus, exercise helps you sleep and feel stronger.

Exercise is very helpful for reducing the stress hormones, like cortisol, in your body and, instead, releasing 'feel-good' hormones such as endorphins. Exercise has been shown to improve sleep quality and helps you fall asleep more easily.

HOW MUCH EXERCISE DO YOU DO?

Say **yes** or **no** to these statements:

- **I do at least one hour of vigorous exercise, three times a week.**

- **I walk or exercise for at least one hour a day.**

- **I enjoy one sport or exercise that I play at least once a week.**

- **I often exercise to feel better if I am stressed.**

Did you say yes to any? If you answered *yes* to more than one, that is good news. If not, do you think that you can increase your exercise or movement at all?

Discuss and think about ways that you might be able to get more exercise and movement. Think of easy steps you can take, like walking from school; or asking to do shopping chores.

Do you think that you would benefit from some more movement breaks during the school day? Discuss this with your mentor. **How could you incorporate more movement during the school/work day?**

WHAT IS *YOUR* WINDOW OF TOLERANCE?

Create a poster to represent what it feels like to be in your Window of Tolerance.

- **Use images, drawings or words to represent what you feel and what helps you stay in your Window of Tolerance. Show the kind of activities and thoughts that help you feel regulated.**

- **Write down some words or adjectives in bubble**

writing that represent what the Window of Tolerance feels like (for example: chilled, excited...).

What do you think you could do regularly to help you stay in your Window of Tolerance?

END-OF-CHAPTER THOUGHTS

☆ How can good sleep help you stay in your Window of Tolerance?

☆ What is meant by sensory overwhelm?

☆ What advice would you give someone who does not do much exercise?

Chapter 3

SELF-CARE FOR YOUR BUSY MIND

How to Regulate and Manage Your Thoughts to Stay in Your Window of Tolerance

LEARNING OBJECTIVES

In this chapter, we will explore the advantages and challenges of having a mind that is often busy and restless. In the section 'What are examples of negative thinking?', we will explore three common types of negative thinking and what to do to change to a cycle of negative thinking.

Would you describe your mind as 'busy' or 'restless'? Does your mind often wander or bounce around ideas?

Many people with ADHD would say that they have a busy mind.

Take a look at the illustration below. **What does it reveal to us about the advantages to having a busy mind?**

A busy mind definitely has some advantages. You might have a vivid imagination or often come up with out-of-the box, creative ideas. Some people call this 'popcorn thinking'. Many stand-up comedians have ADHD. **Perhaps this type of thinking is useful for quick-fire comedy routines and improvisation?**

Can you think of any situations or jobs where 'popcorn thinking' might be useful?

When something really grabs your interest or is urgent, do you find that you can focus on that activity with turbo-charged intensity? This hyper-focus can be very helpful if you need to complete tasks quickly and you may also find that you quickly develop skills or knowledge in these areas that interest you.

Take a look at the image below. **What do you think this image shows us about the possible challenges of a restless mind?**

If you have a restless, busy mind it can be harder to concentrate when you need to or to unwind and relax before sleep. You may find it challenging to filter out and quieten thoughts and ideas, including those that make you worried or angry or overwhelmed. If your mind never stops ticking, you can get stuck in negative cycles of thought.

What *are* examples of negative thinking?

Have you ever spent hours or even days thinking about an event or conversation that upset or angered you? Have you ever hyper-focused on this conversation or event, analysing every detail of what happened? This is called rumination. Ruminating is not the same as reflecting on an event to learn something from it. When you ruminate you simply think over and over the event until your mood and emotions are negatively affected.

What do you think is the difference between reflecting on something that happened in that past and ruminating on it? Why do you think reflecting on an experience may help you reach a better understanding, but ruminating will lead to more negative thinking?

Have you ever spent hours or days fretting about an upcoming event? When you worry excessively or visualize all the things that could go wrong, you can end up feeling quite anxious. This is called catastrophizing.

Have you ever had a very negative, black and white thought? (For example: *'I'm not good at anything. I'm a failure at everything'*, or *'I don't trust anybody. People are all selfish.'*) When your thoughts become too negative, generalized and 'black and white', your perspective will become bleaker. This is called a cognitive distortion.

Take a look at the following sequence of thoughts. **What do you notice about the way each thought feeds into the next?**

How do you think a cognitive distortion could affect your mood or behaviour?

Read through this letter on a problem page. **What event prompted Hamza to think the way he does about himself?**

DEAR AGONY AUNT,

I have been playing football for many years and I *thought* I was a pretty good player, until recently. Last month, I wasn't chosen to play in a really important tournament – instead, others in my team were chosen. I was devastated and I have felt devastated about it *ever* since. I've begun to think that I wasn't ever very good at football and that *everyone* was just being nice when they said I was. I still *enjoy* playing, but this has *really* clouded how I feel about football and I don't even think I will carry on playing anymore.

What do you think I should do?

Thanks,

Hamza

What advice would you give Hamza? What do you think he should do next?

When any of us experience disappointment or sadness, it can colour our thoughts and lead to far more negative thinking. Hamza was very disappointed about not being selected for a football tournament and this made him feel that he should stop playing.

'I'm useless at football. I should just stop playing.'

When thoughts become very black and white, they can feed into more negative thinking until your mood is significantly affected.

We can talk to others about how we feel and also try to challenge these thoughts by using CALM.

What is CALM?

CALM stands for:

C – Challenge a negative thought with a positive, specific example: *'Actually, I am not useless at football – I scored goals in all of the matches I played last season.'*

A – Acknowledge the underlying feeling: *'I feel really disappointed that I didn't get picked for the tournament this time. It's OK to be disappointed.'*

L – Learn to understand: *'I will ask coach what I can do to get better.'*

M – Make plans to distract yourself: *'I will be a bit disappointed for a while, so I will plan to play football in the park for a while and I will visit my cousins next week.'*

How can we distract ourselves?

We can interrupt a cycle of negative thinking by distracting ourselves with enjoyable activities that will draw us away from our own internal thoughts. You may not *feel* like doing anything that could be fun, but taking action will distract you from your thoughts and definitely help you feel better.

A fun activity could be:

- **visiting a new place**
- **skateboarding**
- **starting a new hobby**
- **playing a board game.**

What are your go-to activities to relax?

Warning: Some activities like impulse spending or excessive scrolling can be a distraction, but leave you feeling worse after you finish them. Try to also include fun activities that leave you with a nice memory or skill as this will lift your mood for longer.

Remember!

If you notice that your thoughts are more negative than usual, but you cannot pin-point one event that triggered this, ask yourself the following questions:

- **Do I have too many things happening at home and at school that are upsetting me?**

- **Are there issues with school peers or teachers that I am worried about?**

- **Perhaps I am approaching exams and am getting worried about how I will do and what this could mean?**

- **Do I feel over-tired and stressed?**

In these situations, it's good to get support and advice from people who can help. This could be your mentor, an adult at home or a school staff member you feel comfortable talking to.

You could try this activity to help you 'untangle' and identify what is stressful for you and what steps you can take.

Make a list of all of your worries or what is making you stressed. Write them *all* down, even if they are fears that are unlikely to happen.

Decide which category they belong in:

- **Things I can change soon**

- **Things I cannot change or cannot change soon**

- **Things I am worried about happening in the future.**

With the issues in the first category, it is often useful to talk to someone who can help you come up with a plan of action.

With problems that you feel that you cannot change, for example illness in the family, it is very important to have a support network of people who you can talk to and ask questions or get advice. The following website link can be helpful: www.youngminds.org.uk/young-person/coping-with-life

'Am I a bad person?' How to make sense of unkind or intrusive thoughts

Take a look at the image on the next page.

What do you think prompted Abdul to leave that message?

Have you ever felt resentment towards someone on social media or in real life because their life seems more interesting or fun? What prompted you to feel that way?

The shiny reality presented on social media can convey a lifestyle that appears happier or more glamorous when compared with our own lives. These comparisons may fuel negative thinking and low self-esteem, which can convert to resentment or anger towards the person in the post.

What do you think drives people to troll others on social media?

Trolling on social media or cyberbullying is often fuelled by misdirected anger. It's OK to have unkind or jealous thoughts at times. Your thoughts are not a reflection of you as a person. These thoughts about others often surface because of underlying feelings you have about yourself. To act on these thoughts without taking time to reflect on them can cause harm. Instead, they may help you understand yourself better.

Why do I feel so angry at this person's post? How does it make me feel about myself? What can I do in my life to feel better?

THINKING ABOUT THINKING

With your mentor or on your own sometime during the week, start thinking about your thinking.

Think about the thoughts and mind-wandering you have had in the last two hours.

Ask yourself:

- **Was my thinking focused on what was happening around me or was my mind wandering?**

- **If your mind was wandering, what kind of**

thoughts are you having? Were you daydreaming?
Planning or visualizing an event or activity that
you hope to do? Or were you ruminating, worrying
or in a cycle of negative thinking?

- How did you bring yourself out of the
  mind-wandering?

- Did your thinking affect your physiological
  response? For example, if you were worrying, did
  you feel your heart rate go up?

END-OF-CHAPTER THOUGHTS

☆ What do you think are the advantages and challenges of a 'busy
  brain'?

☆ If someone you know was very self-critical, what advice would
  you give them to feel more positive about themselves? Do you
  think you could follow that advice yourself?

☆ When could somebody use CALM?

☆ What can prompt people to troll others on social media?

Chapter 4

TIPS TO MANAGE RAGE

LEARNING OBJECTIVES

In this chapter, we are going to explore one of the most complicated of all the emotional reactions – anger. We will explore:

☆ *rage* or uncontrolled anger

☆ being very quick to anger

☆ conflict with others.

In each section, we will look at some strategies that we can use to support emotional regulation and prevent the more negative consequences of anger.

When you think of anger, do you think of it as a positive or negative emotion or both? Why?

Anger is an important and necessary emotion. If you face mistreatment, bullying or injustice, or someone has deliberately tried to hurt or upset you, expressing anger can deliver a clear message that you won't accept this kind of treatment. Anger can motivate you to stand up for what you think is right. Human rights and civil rights movements around the world were sparked by people's anger at corrupt or unjust laws.

Anger can be positive, but it has a negative side too. **What do you think this image shows us about the different sides to anger?**

Read this article and discuss the questions that follow it.

ANGER AT THE OSCARS

The Oscars, a film awards ceremony attended by the most famous names in Hollywood, usually attracts press attention for the designer gowns worn on the red carpet, as well as who won what award, but at the 2022 Oscars, a singular action taken by the actor Will Smith eclipsed everything that happened.

Chris Rock, who was hosting, had joked about the actress Jada Smith (Will Smith's wife) and referred to her shaved head. Will Smith's expression changed from laughter to fury; he walked up onto the stage and slapped Chris Rock across the face, watched by millions of people on live TV.

Following the event, there was widespread debate about whether Will Smith had been justified in reacting the way he had. Some suggested that he was simply defending his wife, who suffers from the hair loss condition alopecia. Chris Rock was adamant that he had no idea that Jada Smith suffered from this hair loss condition. And others pointed out that the joke was fairly innocent.

After much debate, the consensus seemed to be that while Will Smith may have had some reason to feel angry, his reaction was too extreme and set a dangerous precedent.

Will Smith later publicly apologized to Chris Rock, but he was given a 10-year ban from attending any future Oscars award ceremonies.

His Oscar win on the night and his highly successful acting career have since been overshadowed by his actions that night.

Did you hear or read anything about what happened at the Oscars? Why do you think everyone was discussing it so much?

Some might argue that the person to have suffered the most from Will Smith's actions is Will Smith himself. Do you agree?

When a strong emotion like anger floods your nervous system, it can be really hard to pause before acting. If you have ADHD, you may find it even harder to regulate your emotion and it will flood your thinking very quickly.

Some people describe this feeling of intense anger as like a mist that descends, clouding all thought and judgement. Anger is a chemical reaction (the fight or flight response), so it makes sense that it feels as if there is a chemical change in the brain!

Anger can become challenging when it is experienced in the following ways:

- **rage or explosive anger** – you may experience very uncontrolled explosions of anger

- **quick to anger** – you may go from feeling OK to feeling really angry quickly

- **conflict and arguments with others** – you may often experience anger towards others, which leads to increased conflict.

Here are some strategies that could help you manage the more challenging outcomes of anger.

Rage = Explosive anger

Task: To begin our exploration of rage, draw a picture that represents *rage* or think of a simile that could represent *rage*:

Rage is like a...

Explain why you have depicted or described *rage* in this way.

Rage is the most extreme form of anger. When anger becomes too extreme, the person who is angry may become physically aggressive and risk causing injury to themselves or damage to property. They may use abusive language or say hurtful things that they later regret. This reaction can jeopardize or even ruin their relationships with others.

Have you ever experienced uncontrolled anger? How did you feel some time afterwards? Did you regret any actions you took?

Even if your feelings of anger are extreme, you will still need to be safe and avoid harming yourself and others.

Read through these situations and identify the examples that show safe ways to react when experiencing anger. You can choose more than one.

1. **Sue's teacher tells her off for throwing a ball of scrunched-up paper in class. Sue tries to explain that she didn't throw it, but the teacher is convinced that it was her and tells her she has a long detention. Sue feels so angry. She:**

a. *calls the teacher a stupid xxxx and throws her pencil case against the wall*

b. *walks out of the room, and paces up and down the corridor outside*

c. *gets back to her task and then speaks to the teacher afterwards.*

2. **At home, Bob's parents have been telling him to clear his dirty plates from his room. He is playing a computer game and is really engrossed. He loses the game and is furious. His mum comes in to his room and tells him off as he hasn't cleared the plates away. Bob:**

a. *throws the plates on the floor and storms out*

b. *runs to the bathroom and shouts that he will clear the plates in 20 minutes*

c. *clears the plates.*

3. **Jamal woke up feeling in a bad mood. He wanted to go to the park with a friend, but his friend cancelled. He is bored and at home. His little sister comes in and starts to tap him on the back and then runs away. He shouts at her to stop, but she does not, so he:**

a. *kicks her and pushes her out of the door*

b. *runs downstairs to tell his Dad to take her away*

c. *tells her to stop and then gets her to play a quick game of cards as she is clearly bored as well.*

It is clear that in each of these situations, the actions depicted in C show a high level of self-control, but it is unrealistic to think that we are capable of this level of restraint, in all situations.

B gives a good example of how someone can manage very strong feelings of anger in a safer, less harmful way than in option A – they leave or find a way to calm down before acting on their rage.

A good strategy to manage feelings of rage is RADE.

What is RADE?

R – Recognize your body's signals

A – Avoid action

D – Distract yourself

E – Exhale deeply

Prepare to use RADE

RADE takes a lot of practice and you may find it hard at first. So, we are going to look at each stage in more detail.

Step 1: Recognize your body's signals

The first thing we need to try and do is learn to recognize the physiological responses we might have when anger feels uncontrolled.

Can you remember a time when you felt really, really angry? What were some of the physiological sensations?

Here are some descriptions of how being very angry feels:

- **My heart was beating very fast.**

- **I felt very hot,** my face felt like it was getting hotter.

- **It was like I was filling up with lava.**

- **My body was tense.** I felt like I was ready to kick or punch. My muscles were tight.

- **My thoughts were flooded with pure anger and hatred.** I felt like I wanted to do something and act there and then.

- **My chest felt heavy.** Like something was tightening over my chest.

Think about the last time you were very, very angry and the anger became uncontrolled. **What was the most obvious physical sign that you were angry?**

It is very helpful to build awareness of the kind of physiological responses you have when you are very angry. This awareness of what is happening internally is called interoception. Developing better interoception skills will help you understand what actions you should take next to help you regulate.

What is interoception?

Interoception is the sense that helps you recognize what is going on inside your body. Interoception helps you recognize what emotions you are feeling and recognize your physical state, for example hunger, thirst or tiredness. Interoception can be more difficult for some people with ADHD, but interoceptive skills can be developed over time as awareness of your bodily states increases.

RECOGNIZING MY SIGNS OF ANGER

Think back to times when you felt very, very angry. **What kind of physiological responses did you experience?** Write out and complete the prompts below.

When I feel very uncontrolled anger, this is often how I feel:

My head feels...

My heart rate begins to...

My chest...

I feel as if...

I want to...

Recognizing the changes in your own body when you start to become very angry will provide you with the clues that you need to implement the rest of the RADE strategy.

Step 2: Avoid

When anger is flooding your system, it is safer to avoid acting straightaway. If you can, always try to leave the scene.

This can feel very counterintuitive.

Anger is a fight or flight response which triggers physiological reactions, such as a faster heart rate and tense muscles in preparation for an attack. If you leave the scene, it will be easier for you to self-regulate.

It can be helpful to think in advance about the places you might go to calm down when you are very, very angry.

HOME

In your home, is there a room or a place where you can go that is quiet and calm? If you share a bedroom with siblings, perhaps there is a corner or area in the house or flat that can be your quiet space?

WALKING

You may prefer to go for a walk. To avoid causing unnecessary worry or putting yourself in unsafe situations, you will need to agree some conditions depending on your age:

- **There may be times when you cannot go for a walk on your own.**

- **Ensure that your family members/guardians are aware that you will be able to calm down.** Discuss and agree this in advance.

Step 3: Distract

After leaving the scene, you may still continue to feel very angry. You may think about what has happened and get even angrier.

When you are very, very angry you will hyper-focus on the reason for your anger. You will be unable to consider the whole situation, and your thinking will be very black and white.

Try and distract yourself from focusing on the event that just occurred by engaging in an activity that will direct your thinking onto something else.

Think of four things that you find often distract you and regulate your nervous system even if you do not have access to a phone or the TV.

Here are some suggestions:

- **listen to music**
- **splash cold water or wipe an ice cube over your face**
- **draw/doodle/scribble**
- **read a book**
- if you are at home, **watch your favourite TV programme** or **play an online game.**

Ensure guardians and siblings understand that when you are very angry, you will need a short amount of time to calm down and you would prefer not to talk. This can vary from at least 15 minutes to 40 minutes. You may need longer in some cases.

SCHOOL

If you are in school, you might be allowed to listen to music with earphones for a short while. **Is there a room you can sit in with adult supervision?** You may continue some classwork after 15 minutes of calming down in this room.

What are your triggers at school? Is there a particular lesson or situation that occurs at lunchtime or break time that often results in you getting angry? Speak to a trusted adult about this, if so. **What modifications could school put in place to minimize this happening?**

Step 4: Exhale

Taking longer, deeper breaths can have a significant impact on your nervous system. Try to do a breathing exercise like belly breathing or box breathing for at least two minutes at a time to help you feel more regulated (see Chapter 8 for more details about breathing exercises).

I feel angry very often, what can I do?

If you find that you need to use RADE often, for example daily or several times a week, then there may be underlying reasons that need to be explored.

There could be too many pressures at home or trauma from your past that is triggering very strong reactions. If that is the case, you may need more intensive support. External pressures and very stressful situations in your life and environment will need to be explored more carefully.

Write out and complete the following RADE plan. Alternatively, you can download a copy to fill in from https://www.jkp.com/catalogue/book/9781839974267

MY RADE PLAN

Recognize
My signs that my anger could become out of control or excessive are:

Physical signs:

Avoid
When I recognize the signs above I know that I could make the situation much worse if I react, so I will avoid acting and leave the scene.

At home, I will go to....
In school, I will go to...
The following members of staff might be on hand to help me...
When I am away from the scene, I will try to bring my anger to a manageable level, so I will aim to...

Distract
I will distract myself by doing one or more of the following activities.

At home, I could...
At school, I could...

I will also try to regulate my breathing.

Exhale

I will try breathing exercises such as box breathing or belly breathing.

Homework

Try to use RADE for one week. Discuss with your mentor or a trusted adult how you think it went. It will take practice and time to become used to using this.

Do you feel you are easily irritated by small things? Perhaps you don't experience explosive anger, but instead get snappy or easily annoyed by small things like how loudly someone is chewing. When you have ADHD, you may have sensory sensitivities that can cause you to feel discomfort. Sleep disturbances or feeling overwhelmed can also make you prone to irritation. **If that is the case, what can you do to help self regulate?**

Quick to anger

Look at these statements and answer **yes**, **no** or **sometimes**.

- **I get angry often throughout the day, most days.**

- **I don't express my anger much at school, but when I am at home, I am often angry.**

- **If I am stressed or worried, then I get angry often, but other times I don't feel as angry.**

- **I often get irritated by things that people do or sounds that they make that they cannot help, like chewing, for example.**

People can become quick to anger for a number of reasons. If you answered *yes* to any of these, it could be useful to try and identify what triggers your anger most often and understand why this makes you angry. Anger is a response to the perception of threat but also to feeling overwhelmed.

Read the script below and consider what you think happened to trigger Bella's anger outburst.

Scene: Bella is upstairs in her room, playing a computer game. The soundtrack from the game is quite loud. Her dog, Jack, is sitting next to her. She looks very focused on the game she has been playing for hours. It is now 10.15pm.

In this scene, her mum speaks to her from downstairs, so she needs to shout to be heard.

> **Mum: (shouts from downstairs) Bella! Have you finished your homework, yet?**
>
> **Bella: (shouts from her room) No! I'll start it in 10 minutes.**
>
> **Mum: Start it?! We agreed you would start it an hour ago. What are you doing?! You've already got into trouble this week for not doing homework! Don't you have a detention already this week?**
>
> **Bella: I'll start it in 10 minutes!!**
>
> **Mum: It's nearly 10.30 at night! You should have started hours ago! Bella? Can you hear me?!**
>
> **Bella: (Bella is concentrating very hard on the game. All of a sudden, the dog barks loudly at something outside and jumps over Bella to reach the window, knocking**

her console from her hands and a drink onto her trousers.) ARGH! Max, you stupid dog!

Mum: Bella! You need to get ready for bed now!! It's really late! BELLA?

Bella: SHUT UP MUM! Just SHUT UP! (Bella gets up, picks up a lamp in her room and drops it, in frustration. It breaks and a shard of the lamp hits the dog.)

Bella got angry in a very short space of time. **In what way could the sounds she was hearing have contributed to her anger?** It is 10.30pm, so quite late at night. **Do you think this will have impacted her levels of tolerance?** She had been concentrating on the game for a long time and was probably in a state of hyper-focus. **How might this have affected her Window of Tolerance?** Use this picture to pinpoint any triggers in the environment that may have contributed to her feeling angry.

There were a number of possible factors that could have contributed to Bella's anger.

- She had **hyper-focused** on the game for a long time, which could have exhausted her.

- It was **late at night** and she may have been tired.

- **The dog knocked over her console** and losing the game would have frustrated her.

- **Her mum was shouting and the dog was barking** – these loud noises at once could have been overwhelming.

> If you experience sensory sensitivity, you can find it difficult to filter out sensory distractions and can become more easily overwhelmed by sensory stimuli in class or at home. This can mean that by the end of the day you feel frazzled and over-tired.

Are you particularly sensitive to any of these sensory stimuli?

- **Itchy labels**

- **Loud noises or many noises at once**

- **Particular smells**

- **Flickering or very bright lights**

- **Other**

- **None**

Bella went on the game to de-stress after a hard day at school, but the game was also engrossing and so she didn't give herself time to relax. It can be useful to try and find different activities to do after a busy day to decompress.

- **Do you have a room or area where you live, where you can feel calm?**

- **What activities do you find relaxing that you can do in the evenings?**

- **If you feel overwhelmed at school, is there a place like the library where you can sit and rest during break or lunchtime?**

- **Would it be helpful to do some of your classwork in a quiet place?** Speak to the SENCo or your teacher about accommodations that are possible and could help you feel less overwhelmed.

If you feel overwhelmed and someone is trying to talk to you or making demands that you don't feel that you can fulfil at that time, use phrases like the examples below to explain to others that you need some time to regulate.

- *'I can't process what you are saying at the moment, I'm too tired. Can we talk about this in an hour/10 minutes?'*

- *'Give me 10 minutes and I will answer you.'*

- *'I just need 5/10 minutes to finish this task, then I will come and hear you out.'*

- *'I am too overwhelmed at the moment. Unless it's an emergency, can we do this tomorrow?'*

- *'If you shout at me, it is harder for me to follow what you are saying.'*

UNDERSTANDING MY TRIGGERS FOR ANGER

Either in the session or for homework, think of a time this week that you became very angry. Consider factors such as how tired or frazzled you might have been and how noisy the room you were in. Here is an example:

Day	Situation/ time/place	Main reason – What made me angry?	Underlying thought or feeling or state	Underlying physical/ sensory factors (tired, hungry, too much noise)
Monday	At home in the evening with everyone watching TV	Sister kept throwing balls of paper at me	I felt ignored. She never listens when I say stop	I had a hard day at school; I was tired; the TV was noisy

After you have reflected on your examples, try to think about what you could have done to minimize your sensory overload or feeling overwhelmed. **Perhaps communicating a boundary clearly and assertively would have stopped a younger sibling trying to annoy you? Did you need to find somewhere quiet to rest?** Look at the examples below of what this person said they could do to try and reduce this happening again.

- *'I need my older brothers and sisters to listen to me and take me seriously when I find something annoying – I need to tell Mum and Dad to tell them to listen.'*

- *'I get very irritated at home by my younger sister.*

I need to find ways to feel more relaxed after school. I find running helps me.'

- *'I need to spend less time gaming as I get very irritated when I lose and I hyper-focus too much and get in a bad mood afterwards. I could try to watch some comedies instead.'*

Write out your own situation using the table as a guide.

Consider what could have happened to minimize the situation:

- **Do you need to be clearer at communicating a boundary to someone? Do you need to do more to relax in the evening?**

- **In school, do you need to ask for any accommodations to support you in class, such as a movement break?**

Conflict

Anger in personal relationships is often a secondary emotion that is triggered by feeling hurt or feeling shame. Past events that were upsetting or scary can trigger a response that is a defence mechanism. This may mean that you get angry or avoid situations that mirror past events. You may feel that you are particularly sensitive to signs of criticism, rejection or perceived criticism – this is often described as 'rejection sensitivity'.

What is rejection sensitivity?

Rejection sensitivity is a term sometimes used to describe an acute sensitivity to criticism, perceived criticism or rejection from others. Everyone can feel hurt by criticism or rejection, but some feel this more strongly. You may seek to avoid situations where you are at risk of feeling hurt and react strongly to any negative reactions of others. Rejection sensitivity may be more common in people with ADHD.

Take a look at the image below. **What do you think it conveys about anger?**

Answer **yes**, **no** or **sometimes** to these statements:

- **I can feel hurt easily by even mild negative comments or criticism.**

- **I react quickly and angrily if I perceive a comment to be critical or negative.**

- **I can become very affected by the comments or actions of others and may dwell on situations for too long.**

If you answered *yes* or *sometimes* to these statements, you may be very sensitive to how others perceive you. This may lead you to react strongly to perceived criticism or rejection.

Read this scene below. **Why do you think Ryan reacted angrily to Sarah? What might have been the underlying motivations for his reaction?**

Ryan and Sara are in the same class at school. They have a friendly relationship and get on well. This scene takes place in a busy school canteen.

> **Ryan has a tray with his food and is about to sit next to Sara.**
>
> **Sara: Noooo, you can't sit here! I am saving this seat for George.**
>
> **Ryan: So? You don't own this seat! I'm sitting down here.**
>
> **Sara: Oi! Can you not??**
>
> **Ryan: Oh, my days! His stuff isn't even there!! How can you save his seat, if he hasn't arrived yet?**

Sara: Just sit somewhere else!! You are soooo annoying!

Ryan: Oh, shut up! You stupid xxxx!

Sara: Don't call me that! You are the most annoying person ever. Just because you have nowhere else to sit, you four-eyed xxxx!

Ryan: Don't talk to me like that, you xxxx. Who do you think you are?!

Sara: Oh, be quiet. No wonder nobody likes you!

Ryan throws Sara's food on the floor. Sara is furious, picks up someone's burger and throws this it at Ryan, covering him with ketchup. It is clear to see how this interaction will escalate further as Sara and Ryan become more enraged.

- **What do you think were the underlying feelings that triggered Ryan's anger?**

- **What do you think were the underlying feelings that triggered Sara's anger?**

- **How and why do you think this interaction escalated?**

- **What underlying thoughts and feelings do you think Ryan and Sara might have had during this altercation?** Draw thought bubbles for each of them and fill them in with your ideas.

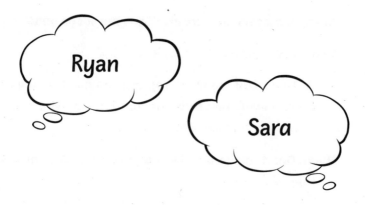

Ryan may have felt that Sara asking him to move was personal, perceived it as a rejection and felt hurt.

What behaviours or actions by others provoke the strongest feelings in us and why?

Sara may have felt tense, knowing that George would be expecting to find a seat free for him as she had promised to save it.

Let's think about how the interaction could be different.

> **Sara: Hi Ryan! Sorry, but I promised George I'd save him a seat as he wanted to discuss something. Would you mind sitting somewhere else today?**
>
> **Ryan: George is not here yet. When he arrives, I will definitely move. I eat quickly anyway. That OK?**
>
> **Sara: Yes, that's fine. Thanks!**

What was different about how Sara and Ryan spoke to each other?

Apart from the language and tone that was used, in this interaction, both Ryan and Sara were careful to explain the motivation or reason for making a request. This can often make a big difference in minimizing the opportunity for someone to perceive a criticism or rejection and therefore helps everyone stay in their Window of Tolerance.

> If we explain why we have asked something or need it, the other person is more likely to understand and not be offended.

Saying that, while we can control and adjust how we communicate with others, we cannot predict or adjust for how others might speak.

Are there particular situations where you often have a strong or heightened feeling of stress or fear?

Read through the following statements. **Which do you think trigger the most anger?**

'I feel that I am being ridiculed or belittled.'

If you have had experiences in the past where you felt belittled, you may have felt shame about yourself (for example, if people responded badly to your excitement or goofing around or if they teased you for not knowing something). This will trigger a strong sense of being attacked when you feel it is happening – even if a comment was intended in a light-hearted way.

'I feel that I am being treated unfairly.'

Perhaps you have experienced being treated unfairly in the

past and feel resentful that this happened? This resentment can stay with you and be expressed in other situations.

Can you recall a time when you were much younger when you feel you were treated unfairly? Do you still feel angry about that situation?

'I feel like I was not in control and I am scared of feeling trapped.'

Sometimes, it can feel that things are happening to you that you have little active control over. You may feel fear that you are being frustrated in some way and cannot do what you need to do. As your attention is very interest-based, you may resent that you have to do more activities that are not interesting to you or are being asked to do something at the wrong time for you. You can quickly feel overwhelmed by too many tasks that are not inherently interesting to you and resent having to do these.

'I feel like I am not listened to and my opinion is dismissed.'

In the past you may have felt that your feelings were disregarded or easily dismissed. **Perhaps you felt your needs were buried to make others feel comfortable?** You may now have a sensitivity to this feeling and this triggers a response of anger even when this is not always the case.

Use the prompts below to help you explore how you might handle situations like this. You can write them out or say them.

When I have to do...I feel...

I worry that...

I feel that I will be...

This makes me...

I may feel like this because it reminds me of...

Now, think about how you might try different approaches in some situations.

Read through these examples. **What is the person doing in each example?**

- *'You don't need to understand the reasons, but I hate it when people call me... Can you please stop? Thanks.'*

- *'I would really like it if you can ask me where we go.'*

- *'I don't think it is fair to ask me to do that at short notice. I'm very tired today.'*

- *'I hear you, but you could have asked me in a more respectful and polite way.'*

If we communicate our needs and motivations clearly, others will understand our boundaries. Clearly communicating boundaries to others can prevent situations escalating when we feel ignored or dismissed.

If you trust someone, it can be helpful to explain why some situations trigger a strong response. For example, certain types of joke or words may hurt you more than people would expect. You might think that they have made a request in a way that is rude or offensive.

Rather than focus on retaliating, you can try to explain what is not acceptable for you.

Sometimes, people may not realize that you feel sensitive about something, because they are not sensitive about it. Being open about certain comments or statements that upset you can help someone understand you better. When we explain our motivations, needs or boundaries in this way, we are assertive and clear.

If you do not know someone very well or do not trust them, and you feel that they may deliberately try to provoke a reaction from you or trigger a response, it is best to make it clear that you do not want any interaction with them.

- *'Do not speak to me. I don't want any communication with you.'*

- *'I have told you many times that I don't want you to speak to me. If you continue to speak to me, I will let the Head of Year know.'*

END-OF-CHAPTER THOUGHTS

☆ What situations do you think cause you the most conflict?

☆ What do you think you might say or do if someone is deliberately provoking you?

☆ If you trust someone, how might you let them know that something annoys or upsets you?

Chapter 5

CONFLICT RESOLUTION

LEARNING OBJECTIVES

In the previous chapter, we explored how to manage anger that is likely otherwise to be expressed in an uncontrolled and harmful way. In this chapter, in the section on 'A simple guide to conflict resolution', we will explore what we can do to resolve or repair a situation after anger has subsided. We will consider how perspective taking can be helpful in the process of resolving conflict.

Anger can be compared to a storm. Some storms are light and with slight rainfall. Other storms are hurricanes that leave devastation in their wake.

If your anger is regulated, you will be able to express yourself clearly to find a resolution. If your anger is unregulated, there is potential for escalation and more conflict.

Unregulated anger may increase the risk of unsafe and harmful consequences, so wherever possible it is helpful to use strategies like RADE to manage that.

EXPLORING THE DIFFERENCE BETWEEN REGULATED AND UNREGULATED ANGER

Take a look at the example behaviours below. **Which do you think indicate unregulated (U) and regulated (R) anger?**

- **You are talking loudly and assertively, but you maintain a physical distance from the other person and are not insulting them.**

- **You are able to communicate why you feel upset clearly and without physical or verbal aggression.**

- **You are shouting very loudly and moving very close to the other person's face.**

- **You have a strong impulse to verbally or physically attack the other person or damage something.**

- **You use language that is intended to hurt and offend someone by criticizing their appearance or character.**

- **You either push, hit, kick, punch or spit at someone or do anything else to hurt them.**

When your anger feels uncontrolled or explosive you are not in your Window of Tolerance and your emotions and physiological reactions are heightened. You won't resolve any conflict in this heightened state. Instead, use RADE or seek intervention from others who are calmer.

When you feel that your emotions are regulated and you are within your Window of Tolerance, you may still feel angry, but you are now able to discuss and find a resolution with the other person. You can begin conflict resolution.

In the previous chapter we read about the conflict between Sara and Ryan.

A few days have passed and Ryan and Sara are calmer. They were on friendly terms before and used to sit next to each other in some lessons. They both slightly regret their actions and feel that they would like to move forward and repair their friendship. Is there potential for repair and conflict resolution?

A simple guide to conflict resolution

Resolving a conflict can be very hard!

Sometimes, conflict can continue or worsen because someone or both parties don't like the idea of backing down or losing face.

'This person is very wrong. This is unfair. I am right.'

DID ANYONE SAY ANYTHING DISCRIMINATORY ABOUT SOMEONE'S RACE, RELIGION, SEXUAL ORIENTATION, GENDER, SEX OR DISABILITY?

YES

When a person uses language that is discriminatory, there are important implications as they have not only insulted and demeaned one individual, but a large group of people.

In this situation, a third party, such as a teacher, must become involved and matters dealt with seriously.

NO

Did either of you make statements that were intended to hurt the other person (i.e. about their appearance or character)?

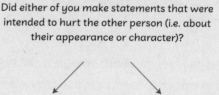

YES

Has this happened frequently or on more than one occasion?

If this has happened frequently, this is bullying or a toxic friendship.

In this case, it is important to let a third party, such as a staff member or another relevant adult, know.

If you are friends with someone who makes you feel bad about yourself persistently, you should try to maintain a distance from them.

NO

If personal insults were exchanged that were not discriminatory, conflict can be resolved, but only if the person makes attempts to repair and apologize for what they said.

After that, the options can be to avoid contact.

Or, if agreed by both parties, they can move onto the stage of conflict resolution.

If no agreement is necessary as this was an isolated case, you can move on.

The value of perspective taking

Listening to the other person explain their point of view and really trying to understand their perspective can be hard. If you are in a fight or flight state, you will not be open to listening to another person's perspective.

Except in cases of bullying, mistreatment or abusive behaviour, many arguments are not black and white. There is often more than one side to an argument.

Instead of arguing for a long time and risking an escalation, sit with the other person and agree that you need a solution.

To help you find a solution, you can use LEAP.

LEAP

To leap, you must:

Listen
Allow the other person to talk for one or two minutes (agree a time) and do not interrupt them.

Explain
Ask them to explain their feelings and what motivated them to feel the way they did. After they have finished, you will explain your point of view for the same amount of time. After this you should both STOP.

Acknowledge

Each should acknowledge some point that the other has made. This shows compassion for each other's perspective.

- *'I can see why you might have been upset.'*

- *'I can see how you might need to...'*

Propose a solution

Any one or both can propose a solution that involves a compromise or fair exchange.

Or: Would it be better simply to agree to disagree?

Perspective taking can be very useful to resolve an argument, but there are times when this is not a good idea. For example:

- **someone has been physically aggressive to you** without any verbal or physical provocation from you

- **somebody has said something to you that is discriminatory and offensive** – for example, they have made a racist or sexist or homophobic comment.

In these situations, there is clearly justification in feeling rage, which others will acknowledge. It doesn't mean that it is the most helpful option for you.

Sometimes people are deliberately provocative to get a reaction. If someone is a stranger, you cannot know how they will react. It is usually better to place a distance between you and that person.

- If you are alone with another person who is provoking you, **go somewhere where there are other people.**

- **Find somewhere safe where the person cannot trigger a reaction.**

- **If someone has made a derogatory comment, make a note of it** (if possible, ask others to record this too).

- Say: *'Get away from me – I do not want to talk to you.'* **Take deep breaths.**

END-OF-CHAPTER THOUGHTS

☆ What is LEAP?

☆ In what way could using strategies like LEAP or RADE help you in your interpersonal relationships?

☆ Think about an argument you had recently with a friend or family member. Do you think you would do anything differently?

☆ When might you need to acknowledge wrongdoing and apologize?

Chapter 6

SOCIAL ANXIETY

What to Do When You Feel Under the Spotlight

LEARNING OBJECTIVES

In this chapter we will explore social anxiety and look at three steps that we can take to improve social anxiety by answering the following questions:

☆ Is this activity important or a necessary part of my daily life?

☆ What do I think is the underlying fear driving anxiety?

☆ How can I gradually build up my tolerance to these situations?

Take a look at the following image. **What is happening? Why do you think the student is so panicked?**

We can all think of a situation when we felt embarrassed and wanted to run and hide, but social anxiety is not just a fleeting moment of embarrassment, it is an intense feeling of fear or anxiety that is prompted by certain situations, where someone feels intense scrutiny. Imagine that everyone is looking at you through a magnifying glass. Social anxiety feels like that is what everyone is doing.

It's quite common for people to feel very apprehensive about specific situations, such as public speaking, but if you rarely face those situations the anxiety you experience will be manageable. However, when activities which are important or necessary in your day-to-day life cause you social anxiety, you will often feel overwhelmed.

If you experience social anxiety, it can be useful to work through the following questions.

Three questions that may help with social anxiety

Is this activity an important or necessary part of my daily life?

Think of any activity that you dread and causes you to experience social anxiety. This might be going to a café, meeting new people or talking on the phone.

Now, ask yourself, is this activity an important or necessary part of my daily life? (For example, if you don't like giving speeches, you could avoid giving speeches, without it affecting your life too much.)

If your answer is *no*, it's probably OK for you to simply avoid this activity.

If your answer is *yes*, ask yourself the next question.

What do I think is the underlying fear driving this anxiety?

If you avoid or fear an event it might be because you are hyper-fixating on any potential negative outcomes. This hyper-fixation will inevitably increase your fear and lead to a fight or flight response.

In some cases, not all, it can be useful to dig a little deeper to find out exactly what the root fear is which lies beneath your anxiety. For example, if your anxiety is provoked by talking on the phone. Ask yourself the following questions in this chart to try and uncover exactly what you dread the most:

Talking to someone on the phone

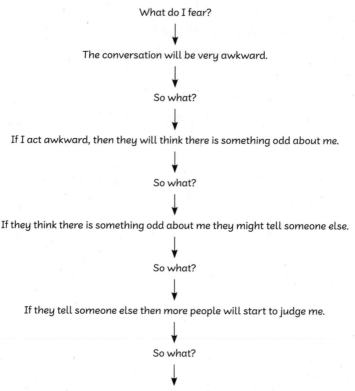

What do I fear?

↓

The conversation will be very awkward.

↓

So what?

↓

If I act awkward, then they will think there is something odd about me.

↓

So what?

↓

If they think there is something odd about me they might tell someone else.

↓

So what?

↓

If they tell someone else then more people will start to judge me.

↓

So what?

↓

If more people judge me then I will be ostracized.

In this example, someone's underlying fear is of being ostracized – left out. **Perhaps they have experienced that feeling in the past?**

The next step is to challenge the cognitive distortion by suggesting other possible and more likely outcomes. Look at these examples:

Fear	Challenge the fear
That person will think there is something odd about me	Even if they do, that is one person. What's so bad about that? Some of my favourite people are unusual and interesting.

That person will tell other people that I am odd	A lot of people will think that person is judgemental because of that. People who know me are what matters.

 Try to follow the same steps now. You can draw out your own flowchart and then challenge the fears based on the example. Or you can download a template from https://www.jkp.com/catalogue/book/9781839974267.

How can I gradually build up my tolerance to the event I fear?

One way of facing anxiety that surfaces in a particular situation is to gradually build up a bank of neutral or positive experiences you've had in the context you fear.

You do this by taking very, very small steps.

When we enter into a spiral of negative thinking, we will become more anxious and then try to avoid being in the situation that we are worrying about. Instead of completely avoiding an anxiety-inducing situation, aim to take gradual steps to build your tolerance in that situation. For example:

Negative association: I hate talking in class because I will embarrass myself.

First very small step: This week, I will answer one very simple question during my favourite lesson.

Second small step: Next week, I will answer one simple question in two lessons.

Third small step: The week after, I will answer a simple question in three lessons.

It might be tempting to rush ahead and do something that is above your comfort zone, but this will only trigger a fight or flight response and might put you off trying again. Instead, take small, incremental steps until you gradually feel safer in that context.

Every time you have tried a new step, think of a very specific example of something positive or neutral that happened. Example: *'I answered a question. Even though the answer was wrong, it didn't matter and no one seemed to care.'*

Gradually, you will build a bank of positive or neutral associations with the activity you feared and fear it less, over time gradually building your tolerance to that situation.

SMALL STEPS TO BUILD TOLERANCE

Think of a situation where you experience social anxiety. Write it down.

Now, decide on very, very small steps that you can take very gradually to build up your tolerance. For example:

Week by week – small step	After the event – neutral or positive thoughts
I will answer one easy question in one of my lessons	Nobody really noticed and I felt comfortable afterwards

Draw out a table like the one above and follow this process to set out and record your own small steps.

Gradually build on these small actions, week by week, and record the neutral and positive thoughts and experiences that you have. As you build on this bank of experiences, you will find that even if one experience is negative, it is outweighed by the positive experiences.

If social anxiety continues to be challenging, speak to a trusted adult, who can help you access further support.

END-OF-CHAPTER THOUGHTS

☆ What are three steps that someone can take to gradually overcome social anxiety?

☆ What kind of breathing exercises might help with the physiological response to social anxiety?

Chapter 7

OVERWHELM

How to Manage That Monday Morning Panic

LEARNING OBJECTIVES

In this chapter, we will explore what situations or experiences can prompt us to feel overwhelmed and how we can use the START technique to return to our Window of Tolerance.

Everyone has experienced a bottleneck moment, when it seems like everything that could go wrong is happening at once. These bottleneck moments can become so overwhelming that a wave of emotion or anxiety washes over you and you cannot think clearly about what steps to take next. Physical discomfort, such as tiredness or lack of sleep, will often increase your feelings of overwhelm.

Overwhelm – hyperarousal

Overwhelm is a state of hyperarousal that can develop quite quickly. Your levels of stress become so heightened that you may cry or become angry.

Look at the image below. **What do you think has led to Emma becoming overwhelmed?**

When you are very overwhelmed, you may find it difficult to take action. When you have ADHD, you may experience these moments of overwhelm due to difficulties with some of the following:

- **timekeeping** – you can find it hard to keep track of time and then find that you are running late or could be late

- **object permanence** – you might often lose or misplace things, so at the last minute you struggle to find items that you need

- **internal hyperactivity** – your brain is always busy. It's a bit like a phone with lots of tabs open – sometimes there are so many thoughts happening at once, it can feel too much to process

- **rejection sensitivity** – emotional sensitivity can increase your tendency to worry about the reactions of others.

When you feel overwhelmed you feel that you cannot take any action; even something like leaving the house feels impossible. You may feel overcome with emotions and feel very tearful or very stressed and angry.

In these moments your mind is flooded with strong emotions, so your priority is to regulate these emotions. Using START can help.

START

START stands for:

Stop
Stop what you are doing.

Time
Time to self-regulate. Pause what you need to do and wait. If someone is waiting for you, call or text them.

If you think you will be late, ask an adult to call on your behalf.

Unless the situation is 'life or death' (highly unlikely), then remind yourself that the world will not come crashing down if you take some time to feel calm.

Air
Get fresh air somewhere quiet or focus on regulating your breathing. Take long deep breaths; count to five as you inhale and count to five as you exhale for at least two minutes. Repeat if you need to.

Repeat affirmations
When you are stressed, you may focus on immediate issues that seem very urgent and all these thoughts will flood your thinking. Thoughts such as:

- *'I am sooo late!'*

- *'I will be in trouble!'*

- *'I will miss the lesson and get into trouble!'*

Many of these problems are not as significant as they feel and can be remedied later and with someone else's help. Repeat the following affirmations, either out loud or in your head:

- **This is not as serious as it feels.**

- **I deserve to feel regulated and calm.**

- **This is not a life-or-death situation. It is OK.**

Take small actions

After some time has passed, you may notice that your breathing is less shallow and you feel less overwhelmed. You can now take a small action, followed by another one. This might be something like do your shoe laces.

Give yourself simple instructions in your head.

- **I will now do my shoe laces.**

- **I will now put my books in my bag.**

- **I will...**

If you become overwhelmed again, stop and repeat the process.

When you have done START and you feel calmer, ensure that you try to focus on what you are doing at that moment. Do not think too far ahead. Instead focus on taking one step forward. If you leave the house, walk at a reasonable pace – accept you might be late now. Look at the sky, breathe calmly. When you arrive, explain or apologize.

Compassion

When you feel overwhelmed it can be very easy to become self-critical. You may think: *'This always happens to me!'*; *'I am useless.'*

Which of these situations make you feel stressed?

- **I get overwhelmed when I feel that I am running late and I am not prepared.**

- **I get overwhelmed when I feel that I have too many things to do and I don't know how to start.**

- **I get overwhelmed when I cannot find anything I need.**

- **I get overwhelmed when I have many people asking me to do something at the same time.**

Time management is a very common challenge for anyone with ADHD. It can constantly feel that time is your enemy. It is very important to get support or to find strategies that can help you with time management. For example:

- **Is there someone in the house who can prompt you at regular times as you are getting ready?**

- **Can you ask for clocks around the house, so that you can see that passing of time?**

- **Be compassionate towards yourself.**

- **Try to give people as much advance warning as possible if you might be late, even if there is a chance you won't.**

Losing things and issues with organization can cause stress too.

One tip is to try to keep important things in open boxes and containers around the house.

What times of the day or situations cause the most overwhelm for you? Is this in the morning? During lesson transitions?

- **Discuss three actions that could be taken beforehand** that might make these situations less stressful.

- **Discuss three accommodations or examples of support from others that may help.** For example, if you often forget your PE kit, can you store it somewhere at school?

END-OF-CHAPTER THOUGHTS

☆ What times or situations make you feel overwhelmed?

☆ When might you use START?

Chapter 8

BECOME A CAMPER AND MANAGE STRESS

LEARNING OBJECTIVES

This chapter explores the effect of stress on emotions and how to spot early signs of stress and burnout. You will learn self-care strategies and the CAMPER approach.

Can you relate to any of these situations? In what way could each situation increase stress levels?

Day-to-day life can seem like an endless list of demands on your attention and time. You have to:

- **get up and go to school on time**
- **remember lots of things that you need to bring or do for school**
- **meet homework or coursework deadlines**
- **pay attention in lessons that you might not enjoy**
- **revise for exams and tests**
- **attend any extracurricular classes you are enrolled in.**

It can feel as if you are constantly pulled between what you want to focus on and what you are expected to focus on.

Your mind might be busy with ideas and thoughts and dreams that interest you. These ideas can sometimes become projects. You can work really hard on projects that interest you and hyper-focus on them.

But you also have all the other things you are expected to do.

This tug of war can be very energy consuming!

The need to refuel

Dr Ned Hallowell, a world authority on ADHD, compared an ADHD mind to a racing car, capable of very fast speeds.[4] Racing cars need regular pit stops to refuel in order to make those top speeds! It is impossible to work to all of your strengths if you don't also allow time to recharge and refuel.

Good and bad stress

When we are stressed our bodies release stress hormones like adrenaline, noradrenaline and cortisol.[5] These stress hormones are designed to help us act quickly under threat. Stress can be really useful for short periods of time. It can help you to think in a clear-headed way, respond quickly to a problem and work more productively on what needs to be done.

But if stress continues for too long you will feel negative effects on your emotional and physical well-being. It can be much harder to relax as you are always on high alert. This will affect your concentration and ability to regulate your emotions; you may experience more outbursts of anger or you may feel anxious or low.

Have you ever heard the term 'tired, but wired'? What do you think this means?

HOW WOULD YOU RATE YOUR STRESS LEVELS CURRENTLY?

Which statement sums up your current stress levels?

1. **I am a bit stressed, but overall, day-to-day life is manageable and enjoyable.**

2. **I feel like there is always too much to do, and I can't get it done.**

3. **I find it hard to relax and switch off and I am irritable more often.**

4. **I feel very stressed and I am often worrying about things. I am also getting angry or tearful much more easily.**

5. **I feel 'wiped out'. I have little energy and feel numb.**

If you said 4 or 5 you may be functioning at an emotional state outside of your Window of Tolerance. Prolonged stress can lead to burnout and lack of energy for everyday activities. Early warning signs of stress or burnout can be subtle at first, you may find it harder than usual to go to sleep at night, or your mind will wander more easily than usual and you may daydream more. People often carry on as usual and ignore the signs. If we are not able to reduce our stress, it builds up.

THE GO-TO STRESS CHECKLIST

It can be hard to recognize the early signs of stress and feeling 'burnout'. Take a look at the stress checklist below and answer **yes** or **no** to each statement.

- **I am more emotionally reactive than usual – I am getting annoyed, angry or overwhelmed by small irritations and frustrations.**

- **I am scrolling on social media for longer periods of time than usual.**

- **I feel really bored most of the time.**

- I am 'tuning out' more often – my mind is wandering a lot and I am daydreaming much more.

- It is hard to unwind at night and fall asleep and I stay awake for longer before I sleep.

- I am arguing more with family or friends.

- I am second guessing myself more in social situations and I dwell on what I said or did afterwards.

- My breathing is shallower – I am taking short, quick breaths more often. Sometimes, I feel my back or head is tense.

- I find it even harder than usual to get started on things I need to do, like showering.

- I always feel like there is too much to do and I am playing catch up.

If you answered *yes* to five or more of the examples on the list, *don't worry*. Instead try to adopt the CAMPER plan for a day, a few days or a week to relax your nervous system and *slooow* your thoughts.

What is the CAMPER plan?

CAMPER stands for:

Compassion

Air

Mindful activities

People

Exercise

Rest

Unfortunately, we cannot always jet away to a tropical beach when we feel ourselves getting stressed! Instead, we have to look at how we can bring down stress levels wherever we are. CAMPER helps with this.

Compassion

Increasing self-compassion and compassion for others stops you from judging yourself too harshly and feeling too self-critical. Too much self-criticism affects your confidence and ability to learn from mistakes and move on. We tend to be harder on ourselves when we get tired and find our performance is slipping. Rather than get angry with yourself, you need to acknowledge that you are tired and be compassionate.

You should:

- **allow yourself to do things you enjoy**
- **reduce expectation to be productive during the CAMPER schedule**
- **prioritize rest**

- **counter negative self-criticism and negatively comparing yourself to others by using CALM** (challenge, acknowledge, learn to understand, make plans). You can learn more about CALM in Chapter 3.

- **not be afraid to ask for help with some tasks**, if you need it. Explain that you are feeling very tired or stressed. Other times, you will be in a position to help others.

- **ask teachers or course leaders for an extension to a deadline.** *Top tip*: If you do this in advance, there is a greater chance this will be accepted than if you ask the day before.

Air

If we are stressed or anxious, our breathing becomes shallower and quicker.

What is your breathing like now?

- **Shallow and quick** – I feel as if I am breathing into the top of my chest.

- **Deep and fairly long** – I feel as if I am breathing deeper into my lungs.

When we are very stressed or very angry or anxious, our breathing gets shallower because the heart pumps more blood around the body to prepare for action. This is part of the fight or flight response that is triggered when our body senses danger. Even if you are not in danger, the response is the same because you *perceive* a threat.

You can help regulate your nervous system by practising belly and box breathing techniques to slow your breathing down.

BREATHING TECHNIQUES

Practise these breathing techniques.

Belly breathing

1. **Take in a very long, slow breath through your nose and mouth for about five seconds and try to breathe into your stomach.**

2. **Watch your stomach expand out – you can even hold your stomach as you do this.**

3. **Then open your mouth and breathe out slowly for about five seconds – watch your stomach deflate.**

Box breathing

1. **Inhale through your nose for 4–5 seconds.**

2. **Breathe out for 4–5 seconds. Do this at least four times.**

During the CAMPER plan, try to do this at least once or twice a day for five minutes or whenever you notice that your breath is shallow.

Fresh air

If we are stressed, anxious or in low mood, we might feel like staying indoors rather than getting daylight and exercise, but some daylight and movement will have a beneficial effect on mood. Even if leaving the house feels counter-intuitive, a short walk will probably help you feel a bit better.

Even if you can't get out into nature, try to increase the amount of daylight you are exposed to. This can be harder in the winter months, but the body's circadian rhythm is programmed to respond to daylight and movement – that is why increased exposure to daylight can improve sleep.

Are you outside for at least one to two hours a day? If not, can you think of ways that you can get movement and daylight?

- **Bike ride or a walk straight after school?**

- **Walking someone's dog?**

Think about how you might fit more daylight or movement into your day, even for short bursts.

Mindful activities

When we are stressed or worried and it feels like there is more pressure on us, we often seek out ways to escape from and numb stress, anxiety or unpleasant feelings. We may automatically seek comfort by 'tuning out' through increased daydreaming or scrolling more on social media.

Take a look at the images below. **Are there any activities that you enjoy? What would you add to these activities?**

Mind-wandering and scrolling can be really enjoyable and relaxing activities (in moderation), but if you find that you are relying on these activities more and more to relax and try to numb your worries, don't worry, but do try to incorporate more mindful activities to help you relax.

What is a mindful activity?

A mindful activity is any activity that is fun and interesting enough for you to stay quite focused, but is relaxing and low-intensity enough that your levels of adrenaline and cortisol decrease and hormones associated with relaxation and pleasure, such as serotonin and oxytocin, increase.

What is a *fun* and interesting activity will vary from person to person depending on their interests at that time. Have a look at some of these suggestions and add any of your own:

- **baking/cooking** – learn a new recipe
- **mechanics/fixing or repairing**
- **art/model making/drawing/craft** – YouTube often has ideas for things to make or do
- **Lego model making**
- **drama or improvisation** – create a short role-play or film
- **low-intensity sport** – avoid very competitive games
- **singing/playing an instrument**
- **sightseeing or visiting a new place** – can you visit a new place in your town or city?
- **knitting/making/adapting old clothes**
- **board games** (only if you do not get very upset about losing!).

Pick three or four activities that you think would be interesting and relaxing for you. When you have chosen, try to schedule enough time for one or more a day.

People

Spending time with others to talk, socialize and enjoy quality time can also reduce stress. This could be family members or friends. It is important that you feel comfortable and accepted in their company as spending time with some people may increase your feelings of stress! Ask yourself:

- **After I have spent time with this person, do I usually feel energized?**
- **Do I feel that I have to try hard when I am with this person or can I be myself?**

If you answer *yes* to these questions, plan to do a mindful activity with this person. When everyone is busy rushing around and getting things done, many of the conversations that you will have can revolve around what you have to do or where you have to be: *'Is your bag packed?' 'What time is dinner?' 'When is the homework due?'*

Talking with others can be cathartic and bring you out of a spiral of worry, but not all kinds of conversations are equal. Share an experience about your day; discuss a funny incident; mention something that you saw or read about; and ask others to share what they think or even ask some advice about an issue or share a worry.

Exercise

What exercise or sport do you do now? Exercise, when your heart rate goes up and you feel out of breath, is really beneficial for managing stress. **Can you do a form of exercise that gets your heart rate up during the week?** Exercise does not need to include going to a class or a structured activity. Any movement that raises your heart rate is exercise. You might go for a run or walk one day and a bike ride the next.

Tip: Think of options that are free and don't require advance booking, as this will feel like a stressful obligation! **Maybe you can agree to go for a long walk or bike ride with someone?**

Rest

There are a few misconceptions about what rest means. Lying down on the sofa is not very restful if you are thinking about all the things you have to do!

In order to rest, you need to actively clear space in your calendar, so that it feels empty of tasks to do. To do this, you may have to:

- **ask teachers in advance for an extension to some deadlines** (if you ask in advance, most people will accommodate you!)

- **postpone or reduce stressful events for a later time** (where possible)

- **postpone an extracurricular activity** (unless you really enjoy it!)

- **ask for help where you can:** *'Can you help me pack my school bag this week? I'll do it next week. Thanks.'*

★ | THE CAMPER TIMETABLE

Copy this timetable into a notebook, or you can download and print out an interactive version from https://www.jkp.com/catalogue/book/9781839974267 – you can refer to it on a regular basis to check your stress levels.

Answer **yes** or **no** to the following statements.

- **I am more emotionally reactive than usual – I am getting annoyed, angry or overwhelmed more easily by small irritations and frustrations.**

- **I am scrolling on social media for longer periods of time than usual.**

- **I feel really bored most of the time.**

- **I am 'tuning out' more often – my mind is wandering a lot and I am daydreaming much more.**

- **It is hard to unwind at night and fall asleep and I stay awake for longer before I sleep.**

- **I am arguing more with family or friends.**

- **I am second guessing myself more in social situations and I dwell on what I said or did afterwards.**

- **My breathing is shallower – I am taking short, quick breaths more often. Sometimes, I feel my back or head is tense.**

- **I find it even harder than usual to get started on things I need to do, like showering.**

- **I always feel like there is too much to do and I am playing catch up.**

I have answered *yes* to four or more.

I will start the CAMPER plan for 1/2/3/4 days or 1/2 weeks.

CAMPER will start on (insert the date).

Compassion

Think of activities, affirmations and thoughts you will have that help you develop a more compassionate mindset.

To show compassion to myself during the CAMPER plan, I will do the following five things on a daily basis:

- **I will...**

- **I will...**

- **I will...**

- **I will...**

- **I will...**

Air

To help regulate my nervous system and slow my breathing down, I will do breathing exercises (belly breathing or box breathing) for two to five minutes:

- **Any time I feel my breathing is too shallow**

- **Once a day**

- **Twice a day**

- **Three times a day**

- **Other**

Fresh air

To get one to two hours of fresh air a day, I will do the following:

On day 1 of CAMPER, I will...

- **Go for a walk in the morning**

- **Go for a bike ride**

- **Other**

On day 2, I will...

Mindful activities

During the CAMPER plan, I will do these activities. (Write down no more than three activities per day.) The fewer activities you add, the easier it is.

- **Day 1:**

- **Day 2:**

- **Day 3:**

Exercise

To increase my exercise or movement, I will try to do at least 5 to 10 minutes a day of the following exercise or movement:

- **Yoga**

- **Fast walking**

- **Bike ride**

- **Other...**

Rest

To clear some space to rest and relax, I may need to ask for an extension or extra time for the following tasks:

I will ask this person to help me with the following tasks:

END-OF-CHAPTER THOUGHTS

☆ What are some signs that might indicate that I am more stressed than normal?

☆ What is something I might do differently after working through this chapter?

☆ What does CAMPER stand for?

☆ When should I try to use CAMPER?

☆ What should I do if CAMPER alone is not enough?

End-of-Book Reflection Questions

★ What strategy in the book do you think has been most useful for you – CALM? RADE? LEAP? START? CAMPER?

★ What self-care strategies help you to stay in your Window of Tolerance?

★ What, if anything, do you think you will do differently after working through some of the exercises in this book?

Emotional Literacy: A Questionnaire

Have another look at the questionnaire you took at the beginning of the book. Answer **yes**, **no** or **sometimes** to these statements again. **Do you think your emotional literacy has improved?**

Self-esteem and self-knowledge

1. **I would like to understand why I get very angry or nervous in some situations**

2. **I am hyper-sensitive about how others perceive me**

3. **I would like to become less angry or nervous in some situations that 'trigger' this reaction**

4. **I would like to understand what I can do to feel less tense sometimes**

5. **I find it hard to get enough sleep**

6. **I don't really understand how sensory or environmental factors affect my stress levels**

Managing negative or intrusive thoughts

7. My thoughts sometimes make me feel very anxious or worried, and I don't know what to do about it

8. I often compare myself to others

9. I would like to learn some ways to recognize and manage negative thoughts

Regulating anger and resolving conflict

10. I find it very hard to control my anger at times

11. I don't always understand why I become so angry

12. I think it could be useful to learn ways to regulate anger

13. I can be quite argumentative

14. I don't really know how to resolve a disagreement without arguing and getting angry

15. It could be helpful to learn different approaches to resolve a disagreement with someone

Managing anxiety and overwhelm

16. I can get very nervous or stressed in social situations

17. I sometimes worry too much about how others might perceive me and this makes me nervous

18. I would like to find ways to feel less worried or panicked in situations involving other people

19. I sometimes get so stressed and overwhelmed in the morning that I cry or don't want to leave the house

20. I often feel overwhelmed by all the things that I have to do

21. I would like to find coping strategies to help when I feel overwhelmed

Recognizing and managing stress

22. I don't really know how to gauge when I am stressed or burnt out until I become overwhelmed

23. I would like to learn different techniques that help me to de-stress and feel more relaxed

24. I often use screen time well into the night to unwind

Tools Used in the Book

CALM

Challenge your thoughts with CALM.

CALM stands for:

C – Challenge a negative thought with a positive, specific example: *'Actually, I am not useless at football – I scored goals in all of the matches I played last season.'*

A – Acknowledge the underlying feeling: *'I feel really disappointed that I didn't get picked for the tournament this time. It's OK to be disappointed.'*

L – Learn to understand: *'I will ask coach what I can do to get better.'*

M – Make plans to distract yourself: *'I will be a bit disappointed for a while, so I will plan to play football in the park for a while and I will visit my cousins next week.'*

RADE

RADE is a strategy that can support the management of rage/anger to avoid the negative consequences of uncontrolled anger.

RADE stands for:

R – Recognize your body's signals. You will need to understand the signs that signify that anger is flooding your nervous system and you feel very dysregulated.

A – Avoid responding. Instead leave the scene. When anger is flooding your system, you will not be able to handle the situation well. All action should be avoided (if possible) until later.

D – Distract. Once you leave, your priority is to bring your strong emotions back to a manageable level. To do this you will need to distract yourself from your thoughts, by doing any activity that helps distract you. This could be walking, playing a game on your phone, reading, etc.

E – Exhale. Breathing deeply helps regulate the fight or flight response in your body.

LEAP

LEAP is a way of resolving a disagreement when you and the other person cannot agree a solution.

LEAP stands for:

L – Listen. Allow the other person to talk for one or two minutes (agree a time) and do not interrupt them.

E – Explain. Ask them to explain their feeling and what motivated them to feel the way they did. Then you should do the same.

A – Acknowledge. Each should acknowledge some point that the other has made. This shows compassion for each other's perspective, e.g. *'I can see how you might need to...'*

P – Propose a solution. Any one or both can propose a solution that involves a compromise or fair exchange.

If you cannot agree, call a neutral person for advice or agree to disagree if no agreement is necessary.

START

When your mind is flooded with strong emotions, your priority is to regulate these emotions. Use START.

START stands for:

S – Stop. Stop what you are doing.

T – Time to self-regulate. Pause what you need to do and wait. If someone is waiting for you, call or text them. If you think you will be late, ask an adult to call on your behalf.

Unless the situation is 'life or death' (highly unlikely), then remind yourself that the world will not come crashing down if you take some time to feel calm.

A – Air. Get fresh air somewhere quiet or focus on regulating your breathing. Take long deep breaths; count to five as you inhale and count to five as you exhale for at least two minutes. Repeat if you need to.

R – Repeat affirmations. When you are stressed, you may focus on immediate issues that seem very urgent, such as: *'I am sooo late!' 'I will be in trouble!'*

Many of these problems are not as significant as they feel and can be remedied later and with someone else's help. Repeat the following affirmations, either out loud or in your head:

- This is not as serious as it feels.
- I deserve to feel regulated and calm.
- This is not a life-or-death situation. It is OK.

T – Take small actions. After some time has passed, you may notice that your breathing is less shallow and you feel less overwhelmed. You can now take a small action, followed by another one. This might be something like do your shoe laces.

Give yourself simple instructions in your head.

- I will now do my shoe laces.
- I will now put my books in my bag.
- I will...

If you become overwhelmed again, stop and repeat the process.

CAMPER

If you are feeling stressed or burnt out, use the CAMPER plan.

CAMPER stands for:

C – Compassion. Increasing self-compassion and compassion for others stops you from judging yourself too harshly and feeling too self-critical.

A – Air. If we are stressed or anxious, our breathing becomes shallower and quicker. You can help regulate your nervous system by practising belly and box breathing techniques to slow your breathing down.*

M – Mindful activities. A mindful activity is any activity that is fun and interesting enough for you to stay quite focused, but is relaxing and low-intensity enough that your levels of adrenaline and cortisol decrease and hormones associated with relaxation and pleasure, such as serotonin and oxytocin, can increase.

P – People. Spending quality time with others to talk and socialize can also reduce stress. This could be a family member or a friend.

E – Exercise. Exercise, when your heart rate goes up and you feel out of breath, is really beneficial for managing stress.

R – Rest. In order to rest, you might need to clear space in your calendar, so that it feels empty of tasks to do.

---

* **Fresh air**
Are you outside for at least one to two hours a day? If not, can you think of ways that you can get movement and daylight?
- Bike ride or a walk straight after school?
- Walking someone's dog?

A Stress Checklist

Use this go-to stress checklist to monitor how you are feeling. You can download a copy from https://www.jkp.com/catalogue/book/9781839974267.

It can be hard to recognize the early signs of stress and 'burnout'. The stress checklist can help you recognize if you are too stressed.

- **I am more emotionally reactive than usual** – I am getting annoyed, angry or overwhelmed more easily by small irritations and frustrations.

- **I am scrolling on social media for longer periods of time than usual.**

- **I feel really bored most of the time.**

- **I am 'tuning out' more often** – my mind is wandering a lot and I am daydreaming much more.

- **It is hard to unwind at night and fall asleep and I stay awake for longer before I sleep.**

- **I am arguing more with family or friends.**

- **I am second guessing myself more in social situations and I dwell on what I said or did afterwards.**

- **My breathing is shallower** – I am taking short, quick breaths more often. Sometimes, I feel my back or head is tense.

- **I find it even harder than usual to get started on things I need to do, like showering.**

- **I always feel like there is too much to do and I am playing catch up.**

If you agreed with five or more of these statements, use the CAMPER plan.

Endnotes

1   Riley, A., Spiel, G., Coghill, D., Doppfner, M. *et al.* (2006) 'Factors related to Health-Related Quality of Life (HRQoL) among children with ADHD in Europe.' *EUR Child Adolescent Psychiatry 15*, 1, i38–i45.

2   Gardner, M. and Gerdes, A.C. (2015) 'A Review of Peer Relationships and Friendships in Youth With ADHD.' *Journal of Attention Disorders 19*, 10, 844–855.

3   Siegel, D.J. (2002) *The Developing Mind: How Relationships and the Brain Interact to Shape Who We Are*, 3rd edition. New York: Guilford Press.

4   Hallowell, N. (2021) 'Your brain is a Ferrari.' *ADDitude*, Sept 28.

5   Henry, J.P. (1992) 'Biological basis of the stress response. Address upon accepting the Hans Selye Award from the American Institute of Stress in Montreux, Switzerland, February 1991.' *Integrative Physiological and Behavioral Science 27*, 66–83.